© 2021 Wendy Berghane
All rights reserved.
Published in Houston, Texas by Bible Study Media, Inc.
Illustrations by Carol Baker
ISBN # 978-1-942243-52-6
Ebook ISBN # 978-1-942243-53-3
Library of Congress Control Number: 2021918871

No part of this publication may be reproduced, stored in retrieval system, or transmitted in any form or by any means electronic, mechanical, photocopy, recording, or otherwise except for brief quotations in printed reviews, without the prior written permission of the publisher.

www.biblestudymedia.com.

Scripture quotations marked (NIV) are taken from the Holy Bible, New International Version®, NIV®. Copyright © 1973, 1978, 1984, 2011 by Biblica, Inc.™ Used by permission of Zondervan. All rights reserved worldwide. www.zondervan.com The "NIV" and "New International Version" are trademarks registered in the United States Patent and Trademark Office by Biblica, Inc.™

Scripture quotations marked (NLT) are taken from the Holy Bible, New Living Translation, copyright ©1996, 2004, 2015 by Tyndale House Foundation. Used by permission of Tyndale House Publishers, Carol Stream, Illinois 60188.
All rights reserved.

Scripture quotations marked (TLB) are taken from The Living Bible copyright © 1971. Used by permission of Tyndale House Publishers, Carol Stream, Illinois 60188. All rights reserved.

Scripture quotations marked (NIRV) are taken from the Holy Bible, New International Reader's Version®, NIRV® Copyright © 1995, 1996, 1998, 2014 by Biblica, Inc.™ Used by permission of Zondervan. All rights reserved worldwide. www.zondervan.com The "NIRV" and "New International Reader's Version" are trademarks registered in the United States Patent and Trademark Office by Biblica, Inc.™

Scripture quotations marked (NLV) are taken from the New Life Version, Copyright © 1969 and 2003. Used by permission of Barbour Publishing, Inc., Uhrichsville, Ohio 44683. All rights reserved.

Printed in the United States of America.

The King Is Coming

Advent Devotional for Children

Wendy Berghane
Illustrations by Carol Baker

DEDICATION

I would love to dedicate this book to the students and families that I had the absolute privilege to serve at St. Peter's Preschool and Kindergarten for ten years. Each one of our chapel times and morning prayers, each song we sang and dance we danced, each moment we shared God's love with one another is imprinted in this book. Thank you for allowing me to be a part of your lives and for igniting such a passion for sharing the Gospel with the youngest hearts. It was a privilege to do so, and I will forever be grateful for our time together!

welcome

Welcome to *The King Is Coming: An Advent Devotional for Children*! I am so glad you picked up this four-week devotional and pray it blesses you and your family.

A little background on how to use this devotional. It was written with a child's heart in mind, so the language and imagery are geared toward them. But it is absolutely a devotional the entire family can use and experience!

Over the four weeks, we will dive into the salvation story by focusing on who God is, the gift of Jesus, and the importance of sharing and celebrating that miraculous gift. There is a short devotional each day and at the end of each week, you will find a few activities you can do as a family throughout the week that emphasize the "theme" of that week. You can choose to do as many or as few of the activities as you wish. I wanted to make it flexible and adaptable for any family. The activities are there to simply enhance learning and growth by offering fun, meaningful, hands-on activities to help reach young hearts.

It can be helpful to set apart a time each day to read through the devotional. Perhaps you can incorporate the devotional into your bedtime routine or make it a part of your breakfast time together. However you decide to use it, I do suggest you read through each day to fully experience the Scriptures and themes.

May God bless you this Advent season as we celebrate the coming of our king!

With love & joy,

Wendy

TABLE OF CONTENTS

11 WEEK 1

25 WEEK 2

43 WEEK 3

61 WEEK 4

Week 1

Day 1
Who Is God?

Have you ever looked out on a sunny day and wondered how the sun knows when to come up and when to go down? Or watched a bird fly and wondered how its wings can get it to soar so high in the air? God created the earth and everything in it. A long, long time

ago he wanted to make a place for his creation to enjoy. So, he made the earth and filled it with such beautiful things! He made the oceans and filled them with fish and shells and whales. He made the sky and filled it with clouds and stars and the sun and the moon. He created mountains and beaches, flowers and trees, and all sorts of amazing animals. (Do you have a favorite?) He also created you and me! God is so

good. And he wants good things for us! He is a very generous God, too. That means he gives us everything we need, even things we don't always know we need, because he loves us so much.

Let's Pray:
Dear God, thank you for creating the world and everything in it. Thank you for being a God who loves us all so very much. Thank you for being a God who is good and a God we can trust. Amen.

"In the beginning God created the heavens and the earth."
- **Genesis 1:1 (NIV)**

Day 2
God is Good!

The Bible helps us get to know God and understand who he is and what he is like. Psalm 25:1-10 gives us lots of words that describe God. Words like loving, trustworthy, and faithful. Those are such good words! This helps us know that God is good, and we can trust him to keep his promises! These verses also tell us that God is a teacher and that he is a God of salvation. That means that he wants us to learn and grow and that he wants to save us from sin (all the bad stuff in the world). What an amazing God!

We are going to learn more about God and how much he loves us over the next few weeks and how he has a very special gift for us—a gift that no one was expecting but one that everyone needs. The gift of Jesus!

Let's Pray:
Dear God, thank you for being a teacher, and thank you for the gift of the Bible so we can learn more about you and Jesus. Please help me get to know you better. Please draw me near to you every day. Amen.

"Show me your ways, Lord, teach me your paths."
- Psalm 25:4 (NIV)

Day 3
God Always Keeps His Promises

Have you ever made a promise to someone? Maybe you promised a friend you'd share a new toy or video game. Maybe you promised your mom you'd clean your room or help her walk the dog. Are you very good at keeping ALL of your promises?

A promise is when we say we are going to do something. It is a commitment or a vow we make to others. We make lots of promises, and although we'd love to say that we are good at keeping all of our promises, the truth is we aren't. We promise to clean our room, but then decide it's too hard or not very much fun, so we don't clean it and break our promise. Or we promise to let a friend have a turn with a new video game, but then we get so caught up in playing it and trying to get to the next level that we never let them have a turn, and we break our promise. Everyone has a hard time keeping promises. Except for God. He keeps every single promise he ever made. He is PERFECT. And when God promises to do something, he ALWAYS does it.

Let's Pray:
Dear God, you are a perfect God who knows how to keep a promise. Please help me make promises I know I can keep. And please help me keep any promise I make so that I can become trustworthy. Amen.

"So let's not get tired of doing what is good. At just the right time we will reap a harvest of blessing if we don't give up."
- Galatians 6:9 (NLT)

Day 4
God is the Perfect Promise-Keeper

The Bible is such an amazing book because it helps us get to know God better and see all the things he has done for his people. There are so many stories in the Bible that show us that God is a promise keeper!

One story from the Old Testament that shows God is a promise keeper is the story of Noah and the Ark. A long time ago (thousands of years ago!), when Noah lived on the earth, people did not love God. They were hurtful and God was sad that his creation had turned against him. Noah was a good man, and he and his family loved God very much. God told Noah to build a huge boat so that he and his family and the animals would be safe. Because Noah loved God, he obeyed God's directions. At the end of the storm, Noah and his family and all

the animals were ok, and they praised God! And do you know what God did? He made a promise to never flood the entire earth again. And he has kept his promise! For thousands of years, God has kept that promise to us!

When God promises us something, he always delivers. God promises to always protect us and work all things for good. Sometimes it might not be in the way we expect, but it is always the best way. He knows so much more than we do and so we learn to trust that his ways are good.

Let's Pray:
Dear God, you are a promise keeper. Thank you for being a God I can trust. Please help me to always trust you and remember how faithful you are. I love you, Lord! Amen.

"Understand... that the Lord your God is the faithful God who for a thousand generations keeps his promises."
- Deuteronomy 7:9a (TLB)

Day 5
The Best Gift Ever

Christmas day is just a few weeks away! Are you excited?! What gifts do you hope will be under the tree?

Did you know that God gave you a very special gift? He delivered it long before you were born, but we still get to enjoy his gift every single day, forever. God gave us the gift us Jesus!!

Jesus is the perfect gift for every single person, and Jesus is a promise from God.

When Jesus was born, he had a mother and an earthly father. He grew up just like we do, starting as a baby, then growing into a boy and eventually into an adult. Jesus had friends. And life was not easy for Jesus. Just like us, he had to deal with mean people, temptations to make bad choices, and even physical pain. He lived in the world just as we do today and experienced all the things we experience. But because he was God's Son, he was perfect. He never made bad choices or did things that were wrong. Jesus is a gift to us because he helped us understand what God is like. He showed us what it was like to be a kind and loving person. He taught us great wisdom. And he helped us understand how big and powerful and mighty God is by performing all sorts of miracles! He could only do this because he is a part of God. Jesus is also a gift because he understands that life isn't easy! We can go to him with our problems, and he truly understands! Jesus is the best gift!

Let's Pray:

Dear God, you are such a kind and loving Father. Thank you for sending your Son, Jesus, to us. Thank you for giving him life so that we can better know you. Please help me grow to be more and more like Jesus each day. Amen.

"But the angel said to them, 'Do not be afraid. I bring you good news. It will bring great joy for all the people. Today in the town of David a Savior has been born to you. He is the Messiah, the Lord.'"
- Luke 2:10-11 (NIRV)

Day 6
Jesus Saves!

Have you ever seen one of these?

It's called a life preserver. Some people may call it a life ring or buoy. But no matter what you call it, it's an important piece of equipment if you are ever out on the water! They don't look very big or strong, but they can save a person who is struggling in the water. That is their purpose: to help save those who are in danger of drowning! They are strong, unsinkable rings and if you are in the water and need help, they will keep you afloat.

Jesus is like our life preserver. We all make mistakes. We all make bad choices and have moments when we love things more than we love God. This is because we are not perfect. We have sin. Sin is not from God, and it separates us from him. God sent us Jesus to save us from our sin. Just like a life preserver saves a person from drowning in the water, Jesus saves us from all our bad choices that keep us separated from God.

Jesus is such a special gift from God!

Let's Pray:

Dear God, thank you for sending us the gift of Jesus. Thank you for keeping your promise to save us from sin so that we will never have to be separated from you. Help me follow Jesus every day. Help me love others the way you love me. Amen.

"She will give birth to a son, and you are to give him the name Jesus, because he will save his people from their sins."
- Matthew 1:21 (NIV)

Day 7
What Does It Mean to Follow Jesus?

God is perfect. He is holy and set apart from all bad things. Because we have sinned (Everyone does!), we are separated from God. But even though God knows we make mistakes, he doesn't want to be apart from us. So, God sent Jesus to be our Savior. Jesus saves us from all the mistakes we made so we can be with God forever.

While we wait for that day, we need to do our best to live like Jesus and trust in the promises of God. To do that, we must make room for Jesus in our hearts! When we decide to follow Jesus, we begin to change. We try to be more like Jesus. We work to be kind, loving, and faithful. We want to read God's Word and tell others about Jesus. We strive to be a good example of someone who loves God and loves others. We try to have more patience and self-control. And we want to focus on good things and not bad things.

Of course, we won't get it right all the time. We will make mistakes. We will make bad choices. But God forgives us every time. We can trust that even when we stumble, God's love for us is so big. We can find strength in that promise to try better next time. God is cheering us on as we do our best to follow him.

Let's Pray:

God, you are my helper each and every day. I can only do better with your help and the promise of your eternal love. Please help me make room in my life for you and for your Son, Jesus. I want to follow you. Amen.

"When Jesus spoke again to the people, he said, 'I am the light of the world. Whoever follows me will never walk in darkness, but will have the light of life.'" - **John 8:12 (NIV)**

Week 1 Activities

- Go for a walk and look at all the amazing things God gave us! Draw or take pictures of some of your favorite things in God's creation. Show your drawings or pictures to others!

- As a family, write 3 or 4 words that describe each member of the family. Have one person read all the words used for each family member. Put these words on post-its or pieces of paper and attach to a bedroom door or bathroom mirror—somewhere you can see the affirmations every day reminding each of you how special God made you.

- Make a Life Preserver Christmas Ornament -
  Supplies:
  White cardboard or cardstock
  2 cups for tracing a circle (1 large, 1 small)
  Red marker, ribbon, or string

  Instructions:
  Using the large cup as a template, trace a circle onto the cardboard. Place the smaller cup inside the larger circle and trace. Cut both circles so you have a doughnut or ring shape. Use markers or ribbon to decorate the ring to look like a life preserver. Write "Jesus Saves!" and hang it on your tree as a reminder of the gift God gave us in Jesus!

Day 1
God's Word Is a Gift

Have you ever received a letter or package in the mail? That can be so exciting! Why do you think receiving a package is exciting? Because it means someone is thinking of you and loves you!

God knew we would need to hear from him in many different ways. So, one of the things he did to help us hear from him was to give us a beautiful book called the Bible. The Bible was written by lots of people who loved God. God poured his Holy Spirit on them and gave them the words to write.

Through the Bible, we can understand just how big and strong God is (He created the earth, sun, moon, and stars just by speaking a word!) and how loving and forgiving he is. God has told us who he is over and over through thousands and thousands of years, but we still sometimes forget. Thankfully, we have the Bible to remind us how much God loves us and also to remind us of all the wonderful things he has done for us and is still doing! The Bible is filled with stories of how God helped his people get through some tough times, and it's also filled with valuable tools to help us get through tough times we might be dealing with today.

God's Word helps us be certain that God loves us and keeps his promises. What a gift he has given us!

Let's Pray:

Dear God, thank you for the gift of the Bible and for giving us direct access to your heart through the stories you have shared. Thank you for all that you have done for us and continue to do. Please help me read the Bible and make it a priority. Lord, help it draw me closer to you. Amen.

"Your word is like a lamp that shows me the way. It is like a light that guides me." **- Psalm 119:105 (NIRV)**

Day 2
God's Messengers

When you hear the word "messenger," what do you think? A mail carrier? An Amazon delivery person? A reporter on the news?

A messenger is someone who delivers something, usually news. They have a message they want to share. God used messengers in the Bible, people who he called on to share his good news!

The Old and New Testament are filled with people who loved God and wanted to tell others how much God loved them. They had so many stories to share about how God worked in their life. They understood what an important message this was to share, and so they did!

God knew he would need a lot of messengers to spread his love all over the earth. He used all sorts of different people to share his message. He used young people and old people, men and women, kings and shepherds. He used people that loved him all their life. And God also used people who at one time weren't very nice. When those not-so-nice people heard about God and saw God work in their lives, they too began to change and wanted to tell others about him! God can use ANYONE to be his messenger!

Let's Pray:
Dear God, you have called on so many kinds of people to share your story from the beginning of time. Thank you for allowing your people to be a part of your story. Help me get to know your messengers in the Bible better so that I can learn from them. Amen.

"I will send my messenger, who will prepare the way before me."
- Malachi 3:1a (NIV)

Day 3
Who is John the Baptist?

Take out a piece of paper and some crayons and draw a picture of what you think this person might look like:

1. A man who lives in the wilderness. (What do you think the wilderness looks like?)

2. He doesn't wear normal clothing, but he wears clothes made out of camel's hair and a leather belt around his waist.

3. He doesn't eat normal meals, but rather lives off locusts (bugs!) and honey.

Does this sound like a messenger of God? Well, guess what! It is! You just drew a picture of John the Baptist, a very important messenger of God. God uses so many kinds of people to share his story!

God gave him the job of sharing the very important news that the time had come for God to send a Savior! John the Baptist loved God very much. He spent his life serving God and telling others about him. He baptized people to help them understand they needed God to make them righteous (holy). But God had an even bigger job for John the Baptist—God wanted John the Baptist to help people understand that God was about to fulfill his promise! This was HUGE news. God's people were hurting. And this was big news that God was going to send someone to overcome all the bad.

But just like John the Baptist didn't seem like a typical prophet in the way he dressed and lived in the woods, the Savior whom God was sending would surprise some people too.

Let's Pray:

Dear God, thank you for using people to be a part of your story. Thank you for all the messengers you have called on to share your story of love. Please give me a desire to read your Word and hear from your messengers. Amen.

"In those days John the Baptist came preaching in the desert in the country of Judea. He said, 'Be sorry for your sins and turn from them'" **- Matthew 3:1-2a (NLV)**

Day 4
God Makes Us Clean

Have you ever gotten really, really dirty? Maybe you played in a mud pile or perhaps you were painting and got all sorts of different color paints all up and down your hands and arms? When you get dirty, how do you get rid of all the mess? You wash!

We can't see our sin like we can see mud or paints, but God can see it. John the Baptist would baptize people as a way of cleaning off all that sin! He wasn't really washing away sin, he was just a person like all of us. He didn't have that power. But he was sharing the message that God was ready to send someone who would wash away our sin and make us clean and perfect in the eyes of God. That person was Jesus! God knew we couldn't be perfect on our own. We can try to keep all the rules and make good choices every single day, but God knew we'd sometimes break a rule or make a bad choice. He knew we could not stay free from sin on our own. So, he sent Jesus to make us clean from our sin. He washes us clean once and for all!

Let's Pray:
Dear God, you are a God full of mercy and grace. Thank you for loving us so much. You knew we would not be able to make all the right choices all the time. Thank you for sending Jesus to clean our hearts from sin. Amen.

"God, create a pure heart in me. Give me a new spirit that is faithful to you." - **Psalm 51:10 (NIRV)**

Day 5
The King Is Here!

John the Baptist had a very important message for God's people. God was ready to send a Savior. God made the promise to his people long ago that he would send the Messiah and restore them (that means to put back together, fix, or make whole). They had been waiting for this day for a long time. But people thought that this Messiah was going to come with great physical power and might, ready to destroy the "bad guys." That's how they thought God was going to get rid of sin!

Can you imagine the shock and confusion when all the messages God sent about the coming of a king were coming true, and then John the Baptist introduced the world to Jesus? This man who was born in a barn. This man who was not wealthy and didn't have any earthly power. He did not come with armies of strong people and big weapons. He didn't use his power to destroy anyone. They all wondered, "Is this really the king God promised would save us? Is this the person who is going to take away the bad and make everything right with God?"

The answer is YES.

Let's Pray:

Dear God, you promised to make things right between you and your people who have sinned. Thank you for being a promise keeper. Thank you for sending us a Savior, Jesus. Amen.

"The next day John the Baptist saw Jesus coming to him. He said, 'See! The Lamb of God Who takes away the sin of the world!'"
- John 1:29 (NLV)

Day 6
Jesus Came to Heal Our Hearts

It must have been so hard for the people in Jesus' day to understand what God was doing. God knew that simply destroying things with weapons or force could never solve the problem of sin. God in his perfect wisdom knew that the only way to fix the problem of sin was to have a perfect king, Jesus, come down and take all of the sin with him to the cross where it would die. Once and for all.

That is such a crazy idea and one that is so hard to understand! But it shows just how wise and loving and faithful our God is. Trying to crush certain people that were the "bad guys" wouldn't fix the problem because everyone sins—even God's people. When Jesus came down from heaven, his job was to clean our hearts so we would love God more than anything else in the world. He fixed our broken and sinful hearts. And that's how God chose to save us. What an awesome God we have!

Let's Pray:
Dear God, you are the God of perfect wisdom. You know what we need even when we don't understand what you are doing. Help us always trust you and your ways. Amen.

"Trust in the Lord with all your heart. Do not depend on your own understanding." - **Proverbs 3:5 (NIRV)**

Day 7
You Are God's Messenger

The Bible is filled with messengers that shared God's story, including the story of our Savior, Jesus. Do you think God continues to work through people sharing his story? If you answered yes, you are correct!! God still uses people, people like you and me, to spread the good news of God's love and the good news of Jesus!

God calls his people to continue to share the Gospel, the good news of God. It may seem a bit overwhelming to be considered one of God's messengers, but it isn't as tough as it sounds. One of the biggest challenges to sharing God's story is simply having the courage to do so!

Joshua tells us to be strong and courageous and trust that God will be with you each and every moment of every day. God does the hard work by opening people's ears and working in their hearts. He uses us as messengers to talk to our friends, family, and others in our community about God as a way of opening a door for him! That's a pretty cool job!

You are a messenger! God can and will use you to help build his kingdom and spread his amazing story of love to others! So, get to know God, get to know his story, and be brave to tell God's story to your friends and family!

Let's Pray:

Dear God, you are such an awesome God who loves his people so deeply. Thank you for allowing us to be a part of your story. Thank you for sending us so many messengers since the beginning of time so that we can know you better. Help me be a messenger for you. Help me know you and give me great courage to share your message with the world. Amen.

"So you must go and make disciples of all nations. Baptize them in the name of the Father and of the Son and of the Holy Spirit."
- Matthew 28:19 (NIRV)

week 2 activities

- Who can you send a message to this week? Take the time to write a note of encouragement to a friend or family member. Tell them how much God loves them. Or maybe write a brief note about something you've learned about God. You are a messenger for God!

- Jesus Takes Away Our Sin Activity - Take 3 glasses or cups. Label one Jesus (larger glass), one Sin, and one Me. Fill the Jesus glass with a mixture of half water and half bleach. Fill the Sin glass with water and add food coloring (the darker the better). Fill the Me glass with plain water. Look at the Me glass with clear water. Say, "This is how we were created to be. Clean and free from sin. But when we make mistakes or bad choices, sin enters our life." Use a spoon or dropper to add some of the Sin water to the Me glass. Say, "Sin changes us. But Jesus came to take away the sin of the world." Add some Sin water to the Jesus glass. The Sin water should "disappear." Say, "He took on all the sin and left it in the grave. He is that powerful. So, when we ask Jesus into our hearts, (Add the Jesus water to the Me glass. It should turn the Me water clear.) Jesus takes that cleansing power and frees us from all of our bad choices. So, we are made clean and pure, just as we were created."

- Countdown to Christmas Chain - Cut strips of paper (one strip for each day left until Christmas morning). Divide the strips among family members. Have each family member write down a truth about God on their strips. (Example: God is a promise keeper, or God uses messengers to help share his story.) Create a countdown chain by linking the strips of paper together using staples or tape. Each day, take a link off the chain, read the truth, and use it in your prayer time (bedtime prayers, prayer before a meal, etc).

Week 3

Day 1
YOU ARE GOD'S DELIGHT

What things make you smile really big? Maybe it's a fun gift like a brand-new bike. Or a day at a theme park. Or swimming in the pool. Or seeing what gifts are under the tree on Christmas morning! Maybe you really love and enjoy spending time with friends or watching a sunset or seeing a rainbow. These are all things that you may delight in—to delight in something means that you really enjoy it.

God uses the word "delight" when he talks about YOU! Zephaniah 3:17 tells us that God delights in us! God loves you and enjoys you. You bring him joy. You make God smile. Not because of anything special that you do, but simply because you are his child, and you are important.

The same verse tells us that not only does God delight in us, but he quiets us with his love. This reminds us that God is our Father in heaven. He is the parent of the universe. And like any good mom or dad, he wants to calm our hearts when we worry or feel afraid. He wants us to live life trusting that he will care for us and help us.

And finally, Zephaniah tells us that God rejoices over us with singing! Think about how much joy and love God must feel to sing over us! God doesn't focus on our mistakes or failures. He simply sees us as a beautiful delight, someone whom he loves unconditionally and sings over with joy! You are God's delight!

Let's Pray:

Dear God, thank you for creating me. Thank you for loving me, not because I make a lot of good decisions or try to be perfect, but simply because I am your child. Thank you for being such an amazing and perfect Father in heaven whom I can trust. God, help me delight in you. Amen.

"The Lord your God is with you. He is the Mighty Warrior who saves. He will take great delight in you." **- Zephaniah 3:17a (NIRV)**

Day 2
God is Your Strength

Have you ever had a really big problem? Something that was hard? Something that was a little scary or overwhelming? Take a minute and think about a time where something was hard. How did you get through it?

The Bible is filled with people who had problems! As a boy, David fought a giant that was WAY bigger and stronger than he was. Daniel was thrown in a den of lions for praying. Paul was thrown in prison for telling people about Jesus! And people's problems did not end with the writing of the Bible. They continued and still continue today. But so does God. God was with David and Daniel and Paul during those times of trouble, and he gave them the strength they needed to persevere. And that same God is with you! God is your strength!

Sometimes God's strength will look like a miraculous power as it did with David beating Goliath. Sometimes it will look like a taming or quieting of a situation like it did with Daniel and the lions. Sometimes God's strength will look like patience and perseverance, like it did with Paul. God promises us his strength. He doesn't want us to face battles alone. He loves us, rejoices over us, and wants us to learn to lean on him so we can be made stronger.

What a great reminder that God is where we get our strength! We can trust that no matter what problems arise, we have all we need to get through because God is with us.

Let's Pray:

Dear God, you are a God of strength! You have helped your people with all sorts of problems since the beginning, and I am so glad you are here to help me! Help me remember that you are my strength. When I have a problem, I can come to you for help, and you will get me through. Amen.

"Here is what I am commanding you to do. Be strong and brave. Do not be afraid. Do not lose hope. I am the Lord your God. I will be with you everywhere you go." **- Joshua 1:9 (NIRV)**

Day 3
No Need to Worry

Have you ever watched a bird build a nest? They fly around looking for material, and it's amazing to see what they can use! They collect pine needles, twigs, hay, grass, and maybe even mud to help build a safe and sturdy nest to call home. They never lack building materials.

Have you ever seen a squirrel look for food? They always find delicious treats no matter where they are. They eat acorns, flowers, fruit, and nuts—they never go hungry.

The Bible tells us that God loves the squirrels and birds and provides for them. Each day they are given what they need. The verse goes on to remind us how much more important and loved we are by God than squirrels and birds! And if he provides for them, we can trust that he will provide for us.

God doesn't want us to worry. When we worry, it steals our peace and makes it hard for us to see and enjoy all the things God has provided. Worry leads to focusing on things that are out of our control. God wants us to trust him and his promise to give us what we need, when we need it. He loves us too much to want us to worry about things. He simply wants us to trust his promises!

Let's Pray:

Dear God, you love your creation, every part of it. You take care of the animals and flowers, and you most certainly take care of me. Help me always remember how important I am to you and trust you with all things. Help me not to worry, but instead hold on to your promise to give us what we need, when we need it. Amen.

"Don't worry about anything; instead, pray about everything. Tell God what you need, and thank him for all he has done."
- Philippians 4:6 (NLT)

Day 4
God is Not Finished

God continues to work in and through his people. God chose you to be a part of his family, and he will continue to work in your life, in your mind, and in your heart. He is working in you each time you recognize something beautiful that he's given you. He is working in you when you talk to him and pray. He is working in you when you go through some tough times. He is always helping you grow, always helping you learn, and always working to shape your heart to look like the heart of Jesus.

God works through you, too! Every time you help someone, serve, volunteer, or treat people with love and kindness, you are doing God's work. Each time you thank people for their help or encourage someone to not give up, you are spreading God's love! God uses people to do some of his work on earth. We are all a part of sharing God's love and pointing people to Jesus!

God's work is not finished. The gift he gave us in Jesus helps us continue to grow and learn and be a part of God's kingdom work. God isn't finished working in us, and he isn't finished working in the world!

Let's Pray:

Dear God, we praise you for all that you do in the world and in our lives. Sometimes it's easy to forget that you are still very much alive and working in and through your people. Even when the world seems scary, you are still there. Thank you for being in my life and continuing to shape my heart. Help me be a light to the world by trying my best to live like Jesus. Amen.

"He said to them, 'My Father is always doing his work. He is working right up to this day. I am working too.'" **- John 5:17 (NIRV)**

Day 5
The Gift of True Joy

Do you know the famous Christmas hymn that says, "Joy to the world, the Lord has come! Let earth receive her king! Let every heart prepare him room, and heaven and nature sing!"?

Joy is an awesome word. But sometimes people confuse the word joy with happiness. They are not the same. Joy is not based on things or people or places. Those things can make you happy for a minute or two, but they fade away or let you down, and you are right back where you were, looking for something else to make you feel good.

Joy is different. Joy is a feeling of contentment and peace in all circumstances because you know God is good. Joy flows from your heart when you trust in the promise of Jesus because you know that no matter what happens—all the good and the bad—it never changes the fact that you are a child of God. Through Jesus, God has made you his child. That is JOY!

Joy is a powerful thing. It is steady. It is sure. It brings peace, and it changes hearts. God's presence brings a joy that casts out fear because at the end of the day you trust that God will never leave you, and one day you will be sitting next to him and will feel a love and safety that is simply unfathomable.

So sing it loud, friends! JOY TO THE WORLD!!!

Let's Pray:

Dear God, thank you for the promise of your Son, Jesus. Thank you for giving us joy each day just by knowing you. Please help us love you and open our hearts each day to your teaching and love. We love you Lord. Amen.

"But the Holy Spirit produces this kind of fruit in our lives: love, joy, peace, patience, kindness, goodness, faithfulness, gentleness, and self-control." **- Galatians 5:22-23a (NLT)**

Day 6
What Does It Mean to Share God's Love?

God loves you so very much. The love he has for you is bigger than the entire universe. He loves you more than the sun and moon and sky. He loves you more than all the grains of sand on every beach and more than all the animals on earth. His love for you is so huge and so perfect. It is immense. In fact, his love for you is so abundant that there is plenty to share with others, and that's just what he wants you to do!

Luke 3:10-14 reminds us that we should share with others, treating people as worthy of our help and love. And once we understand how much God loves us and how awesome our God is, our natural reaction is to share his love with everyone!

What does sharing God's love look like? It looks like:
- A smile
- Words of encouragement
- Helping someone
- Being grateful
- Praying for others
- Forgiving others when they make mistakes
- Approaching a problem with calmness and self-control
- Letting others know how much God loves them

Anyone can share God's love. And the cool thing is, when you work to share God's love with others, Jesus works in your heart, making it more like his. It's a win-win! You can make a difference in someone's life, and God changes yours!

Let's Pray:
Dear God, you have shown us every day how much you love us. Help us share your love with others. Thank you for giving us the opportunity to be part of your story by spreading your message. Amen.

"John answered, 'Anyone who has extra clothes should share with the one who has none. And anyone who has extra food should do the same.'" **- Luke 3:11 (NIRV)**

Day 7
GOD'S BIG LOVE

Sharing God's love comes from understanding how much God loves us. Through Jesus, God is able to shower us with grace and forgiveness. When we make mistakes, when we make bad choices, when we get stuck in bad habits, God's love and grace cover us. Because of Jesus, God doesn't see our faults. He just sees us as his amazing children, filled with love and beauty. We don't deserve to be looked at this way, but it's how God sees us. He sees us as forgiven. He sees us as clean. That is love. And the really cool part is that we can share that love by showing the same grace when others make mistakes. We can still love people when they make a bad choice. We can love others the way God loves us. We won't always do it perfectly, but that's ok. Because when we try to love others like this, it creates joy in our hearts. That feeling of peace that no matter what mistakes you make, or people make, God still loves us and cares for us and is here to help us.

Let's Pray:

Dear God, you are love and you are joy. Help me love like you. Help me find such joy in who you are that other people will want to know you too. Amen.

"Here is my command. Love one another, just as I have loved you."
- John 15:12 (NIRV)

Week 3 Activities

- As a family, listen to a couple different versions of the hymn "Joy to the World." Which is your favorite? Talk about how the promises of God bring joy to your heart!

- What is an activity that you delight in (really enjoy) as a family? Plan a time to do that activity together, and put it on the calendar! Take time to delight in the gift of each other, and thank God for delighting in you!

- Think of ways you can share God's love with others. Is there a neighbor who could use help with their yard work? A new mother you could make dinner for? An organization you could volunteer with as a family? Choose a way to serve others and share God's love this week!

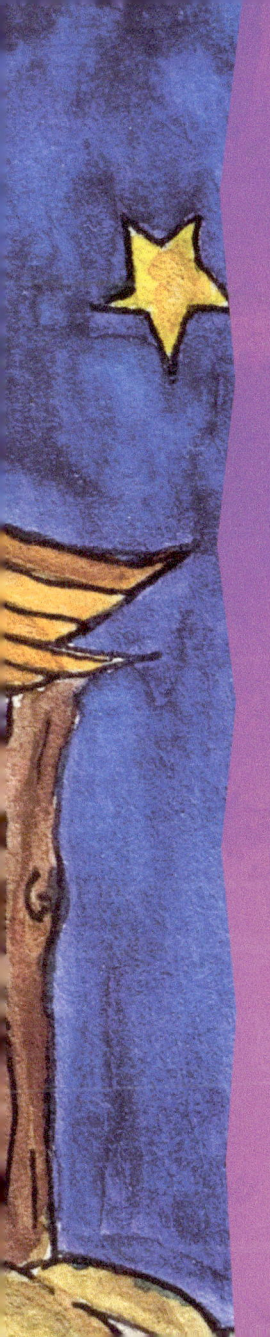

Week 4

Day 1
Praise God!

How does it feel when someone tells you that you are awesome? When they notice the hard work you've put into schoolwork or chores? Or when someone thanks you for your help? Encouragement and praise feel really good. Especially when you've worked hard to do something special.

Just as we like to hear people praise us, God likes to hear praises, too! David tells us in Psalm 150:6 that everything that has breath should praise the Lord!

The thing is, God doesn't need our praise. He is completely self-sufficient. That means he doesn't need any help with anything because he is perfect in every way. He is God! So, he doesn't need us to praise him, but he is certainly worthy of our praise!

God tells us to praise him because it is such a wonderful way for us to be reminded of all the wonderful ways that God provides. Praising God sets our hearts and minds on the right track and helps us notice all the good around us. Praising God helps us focus on how amazing and powerful and faithful God is and how generous he has been to us. When we praise God, it also helps get us excited about God, which is so good for our hearts!

Even though God tells us we should praise him, it's not really about him! He knows when we set our hearts towards praising him, it helps us see the good in the world and the good that he provides. He wants our hearts and minds to be focused on the good stuff, not on things like fear or worry. Isn't that amazing? That even praising God is really about his love for us! That is definitely worth praising!

Let's Pray:

God, you are so good, and we want to praise you! Thank you for giving me the eyes to see all the amazing things in this world. Help me always focus on you, God. Amen.

"Let everything that has breath praise the Lord! Praise the Lord!"
- Psalm 150:6 (NIRV)

Day 2
Mary's Song of Praise

There are many beautiful examples of people praising God all through the Bible. One of them is found in the Gospel of Luke, chapter 1, where Mary is praising God! She just found out that she was chosen to be the mother to Jesus. I'm guessing she felt excited and probably very scared and confused, too. This was a big job! But even in her worry and fear, she praised God. She focused on all the good things God was doing, not only in her life but in the lives of everyone.

Mary believed with all her heart that God would care for her, protect her, and lead her and her family. She knew she was blessed, not just with things, but because she understood the goodness of God and how she was a part of his story. You are part of his story, too! Your role is different than Mary's, of course, but it is no less special and unique and important! God has a great plan for each of us. He created us to be a part of his story. We are all blessed because God created us with beautiful intention.

So, celebrate that, friends! Praise God for making you for a purpose! Sing to him, pray to him, glorify his name knowing that you are blessed. Not because of all the things you have, but because of who you are as a child of God!

Let's Pray:

Dear God, you are a God who loves us and created us for a purpose. Help me remember that I am your child, and you know me by name. Help me grow into the gifts and strengths you have given me. I am blessed because I am important to you! Amen.

"Mary said, 'My soul gives glory to the Lord. My spirit delights in God my Savior. The Mighty One has done great things for me. His name is holy.'" **- Luke 1:46-47; 49 (NIRV)**

Day 3
How Can You Worship God Today?

Mary praised God because she believed in God's goodness. Like Mary, we can see all that God has done for us and celebrate because we are so loved by him. Sometimes it's really tough to understand God and his big love for us. And that's ok. Because we are people and not God, it is impossible for us to fully understand him. But we can see the goodness that he brings into our lives. And we can love and follow Jesus knowing that he is our Savior. Then we can praise and worship God like Mary did!

There are many ways to worship: we can go to church, sing songs to God, and pray to him. Some people even play music or dance for God in their worship! These are all great ways to worship! The most important thing about worship is that it comes from the heart. It's not about putting on a show or wanting people to praise you. When we worship, it should be about God and his Son Jesus.

So, praise God today! Worship the Lord for all that he has done and will do! Sing, dance, pray! Tell God how incredible he is and thank him for his love!

Let's Pray:

God, you are the creator of the stars and the sun, the birds, and the fish, and you are the creator of me. My heart is so full because you love me so much. Draw me closer to you every day, and help me remember that you are worthy of worship and praise! Amen.

"Worship the Lord with gladness. Come to him with songs of joy."
- Psalm 100:2 (NIRV)

Day 4
The Gift of Jesus

God is so good. That is a truth that we have been reminded of time and time again on this Advent journey. He has provided us with so much, including the best and most undeserved gift we could ever be given, the gift of Jesus.

God is so good to us and loves us so very much that he doesn't ever want to be without us! But there was a problem. You see, God is perfect and holy. That means he cannot be sinful. He cannot make wrong choices. But we can. And we do. We sometimes make decisions that are not good. We sin. And sin cannot be with God.

But friends, here is the GOOD NEWS. Even though we are sinful and make bad choices, God didn't want to let us suffer in sin forever. God promised to not let us go, so he sent Jesus to save us and take all our bad choices and wash them away! Isn't that amazing!! God loves us that much, friends. He wants us never to be apart from him. And he knew we couldn't do that on our own. So, he gave us Jesus. What a beautiful gift. God is so good.

Let's Pray:

Dear God, you are a perfect and holy God. You are without sin and full of love. Thank you, God, for promising to never be separated from us. Thank you for sending your Son, Jesus to take our sin away. Please work in our hearts so that we can be more and more like Jesus each day. Amen.

"Everyone who calls on the name of the Lord will be saved."
- Romans 10:13 (NIRV)

Day 5
Will You Accept the Gift of Jesus?

Have you ever been given a gift? What happens when someone gives you something special? Do you keep it on the shelf, all wrapped up? Do you give it back? Usually when someone gives you a special gift, you accept it and thank the person for being so kind and thoughtful!

Yesterday we talked about how God loves us so much that he never wants us to be apart from him. So, he sent us Jesus. Jesus is a gift to us!

God gave us the gift of Jesus, and we need to accept that gift. When we begin to understand that we are not perfect and need Jesus to wipe away those bad choices we make, then we are able to start having a friendship with Jesus. We can call on him, just like we call on God. We can read about him in the Bible and try to follow his example of loving others, being kind, and always keeping God first in his heart. God sent Jesus to be our friend, to help us make better choices (although we won't ever be perfect), and to make us whole again. When we welcome Jesus into our life, we are restored! That means God doesn't see all the broken pieces in our lives. Instead, he sees us the way he created us, beautiful and without sin. Jesus is the gift that makes that possible.

That is so much to think about! And so incredibly special!

Let's Pray:

God, thank you for Jesus. Thank you for giving us the gift of your perfect Son. Thank you for loving us so much that you were willing to do whatever it takes to have us in your perfect and holy kingdom. Please move my heart to accept Jesus as my Savior. Amen.

"God so loved the world that he gave his one and only Son. Anyone who believes in him will not die but will have eternal life."
- John 3:16 (NIRV)

Day 6
God's Love for You Never Changes!

As Christians, we are adopted into God's family! God chose us to be his children. Not because of anything we've done, but simply because he loves us! And there is even better news: nothing will ever change that because God doesn't change! What a relief to know that no matter what, God's love for us will never change! That is worth celebrating!

The God that created the earth is the same God that created you. The God that loved Noah and Moses is the same God that loves you. The God that sent his Son down from heaven is the same God that wants to be with you. His love doesn't change. His character doesn't change. His faithfulness doesn't change. It doesn't matter what we do. When we accept Jesus as our Savior, then nothing we do or don't do will ever separate us from his love.

People change all the time. They change their minds, and sometimes they even change the rules. They break promises. But we can always count on God. Through life's ups and downs, we can be sure that God loves us, delights in us, and created us for a purpose. God does not change. His promises do not change. His love for us does not change. Ever.

Friends, let's believe that with all of our hearts!

Let's Pray:

God, in a world that seems to change all the time, we know you do not change. Your love for us will never go away, no matter what. Your promises will never be broken. Thank you for being a God that does not change. Amen.

"I the Lord do not change." **- Malachi 3:6a (NIV)**

Day 7

Celebrating the Gift of Jesus!

Friends, it is almost Christmas Day! The day we celebrate the birth of Jesus! We have learned so much about God and his promises during Advent. We have learned that he is such a good God who gives us so much. We have learned that God is faithful and never breaks his promises. We discovered that Jesus is God's gift to us so that we don't ever have to be separated from him! And most of all, we have learned that God loves us so very much.

As you celebrate Christmas with your family and friends, don't forget what the story of Jesus is really all about. Jesus is a promise from God, a promise that comes with so much love. He is a gift for you and for me.

So, remember to praise God today, tomorrow, and every day! Thank him for the earth, the animals, and all of creation! Tell him what an awesome job he has done! Praise him for all the things he gives you: strong legs to run and jump, a mind to think, and a purpose he had for you when he created you. Tell God just how much you love him! Worship him with singing and dancing! Thank him for the gift of Jesus! Thank him for being a promise keeper and never changing. God is so good!

Let's Pray:

God, thank you for helping me learn more about you over this Advent season. Help me take what I've learned and keep it in my heart and mind. Help me believe in you and in your Son Jesus every single day. Amen.

"I have hidden your word in my heart that I might not sin against you." - **Psalm 119:11 (NIV)**

Week 4 Activities

- Have a birthday party for Jesus complete with cupcakes, balloons, and streamers! Thank God for the gift of Jesus, for his promise to send us a Savior. Celebrate Jesus this week!

- Take a current family picture and have it printed. Talk about a strength that each family member has. How has God gifted that family member? On the back of the picture, write down each family member and their strength. Using craft sticks, create a frame for your picture. (You could also make a paper plate frame or research other homemade frame ideas.) Thank God for uniquely making each family member, and pray for God's help in using those gifts to bring goodness and love into the world!

- Memorize Psalm 100:2: *"Worship the Lord with gladness! Come before him with joyful songs!"* Add motions to the words to make it easier to remember and more fun to say with others.

ACKNOWLEDGEMENTS

I was flooded with emotion as I completed this devotional (which is my very first published book!). I felt relieved, excited, and scared, but most of all I felt incredibly blessed. I am so humbled and, quite honestly, in absolute awe that our very good Father led me to a place where this was a possibility. There are so many people that helped me get here that I want to honor:

My family, especially my husband, Steve, and my two kids, Nick and Abby, for their endless support and encouraging me to follow my dreams.

My dear friend Brooke for helping me put this in motion and for being a mentor in the writing process as well as one of my biggest cheerleaders.

The entire team at Bible Study Media and my awesome friends Wes and Tom for helping me with all the edits and Scripture studies.

And a huge thanks to my mom, Carol, for sharing her gift and creating the amazing illustrations for this book.

An Advent book so meaty you'll need a steak knife to get through it.

Advent waits for the return of Christ, not his birth. It's about judgment turned to grace, faith to sight, exile to home. It's about prophecy and promise as told by heavy hitters like David, John the Baptist, Mary and Micah, Elizabeth and Zechariah. Advent is not a snack to tide you over. It's not an appetizer. Advent is the meal.

What is shaping your child's heart and mind?

HEARTS ALIVE

Sunday School

Fall
Winter
Spring

HEARTS ALIVE

Children's Church

Fall
Winter
Spring
Summer

THE CROSS WALK

Our children's curriculum collection molds hearts and captivates minds by introducing children to God through his Word. It will ignite their hearts and engage their young minds with the story of salvation and how it ties to a personal relationship with their Savior Jesus Christ.

Bible Study Media

Igniting Hearts. Engaging Minds.

biblestudymedia.com   info@biblestudymedia.

Bible study reimagined.

Introducing an online comunity at ignite.biblestudymedia.com.

Ignite was created so that you can study the Bible at any time, in any place, with a global community of believers. **Connect today.**

www.ingramcontent.com/pod-product-compliance
Lightning Source LLC
Chambersburg PA
CBHW041131110526
44592CB00020B/2768